LORENA PAJALUNGA

Good Night Yoga

Relaxing Bedtime Poses for Children

ILLUSTRATIONS BY ANNA LÁNG

WSKids
WHITE STAR KIDS

INTRODUCTION

The word yoga derives from the root *yuj*, "to bind together," "to unite," "to keep close;" so, in yoga the action of binding and connecting must allow the person who practices it to reunite all the opposites harmoniously. The body and the consciousness, the individual and the universe, the head and the heart, breathing and sensations, psyche and memory, activity and passivity, will and abandonment must all come together.

Traditional, classic Ptanjali yoga is a path, a methodology and a philosophy in which the *asana*, that is the positions, are only a small part of what leads

to the understanding of self, which takes different names according to the cultures and the traditions. It is precisely thanks to the poses that we can interest children and help them to explore the world of yoga, transmitting important messages and values that this ancient discipline has been teaching for thousands of years.

In my experience, children have an extraordinary capacity for going beyond the bodily, basic aspect of the *asana*, immediately and instinctively understanding the energetic and symbolic aspect of the pose they are shown. . . allowing the true essence of the practice of yoga to emerge effortlessly.

This book was born from the all too familiar difficulties that bedtime can involve for parents and for small children, who are bursting with energy and do not see any reason for winding down, experiencing rest and sleep as an imposition.

Bedtime yoga is intended to offer a way, a ritual to accompany the child towards an appropriate sense of relaxation, calm and serenity so that he/she can face going to bed without a fuss. I have chosen poses that gently relax the body and the mind into a state of serene abandonment, evoking the sensations of peace and tranquility linked to nighttime.

IT'S TIME TO GO TO SLEEP

"It's time to go to sleep", says Pops, looking into the children's bedroom, but Anna and Theo immediately protest: they can't go to sleep, there are too many thinks to do!

"My train is ready for a journey," explains Theo. "My lion wants to drive the train," he says, pointing to his favorite soft toy: a lion with a cute face and an untidy mane.

"What about my tower? I can't stop building it now!" exclaims Anna angrily. "I promised my teddy bear that we could climb it together!" Anna shows her father the teddy bear she is cuddling.

Explanations and protests are all in vain: father smiles and mother gives them a kiss before the door of the bedroom closes quietly.

"I am not going to sleep, Anna! I will not close my eyes all night long!" Theo says to his sister.

"Nor me. I don't want to say goodnight to our toys and I can't sleep when I'm upset."

"We have the solution for that," says a little voice.

The two children are not alarmed when they see that it was their panda who was speaking: in their imagination all the toys come to life, talk, laugh and move around, it's not at all strange! What they did not expect was that the panda would tell them next.

"We all know a secret, a special pose, rather magical, that if you do it correctly will help you to rest. It will take away all the anger and the tiredness."

"It will be fun," says Theo's lion. "We'll start, just watch!"

The MOUNTAIN
Pose

TADA-ASANA

THE MOUNTAIN POSE IS A MAGNIFICENT POSITION, SUITED TO THE KING OF ANIMALS! STAND BESIDE ME AND I WILL SHOW YOU. STAND UP STRAIGHT WITH YOUR LEGS SLIGHTLY PARTED. KEEP YOUR BACK VERY STRAIGHT! NOW PLACE YOUR ARMS BY YOUR SIDES, YOUR FINGERS POINTING TO THE GROUND. REMAIN VERY STILL AND LET ME LOOK AT YOU: YOU LOOK JUST LIKE A MOUNTAIN!

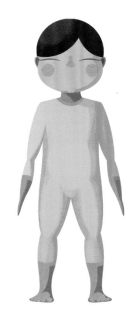

1

Stand with the feet slightly apart. (The distance between the feet must correspond to that of the pelvis).

2

Spread the arms with the fingers pointing towards the ground. Close the eyes and remain absolutely still for a few moments, like a huge mountain.

The lion has shown me how, just like a mountain, I can be strong also when I remain calm.

The BEAR Pose

JAMBAVAT-ASANA

IT IS EASY TO MOVE FROM THE MOUNTAIN POSE TO THE ONE THAT BEARS MY NAME. LET'S TRY IT TOGETHER! FIRST OF ALL, TRY TO IMAGINE THAT YOUR FEET HAVE BECOME BIG PAWS, RESTING FIRMLY ON THE GROUND. NOW BEND YOUR KNEES AND EXTEND YOUR ARM IN FRONT OF YOU, KEEPING YOUR FINGERS WIDE OPEN AND A LITTLE CURVED, LIKE THE PAWS OF A HUNGRY BEAR READY TO STEAL SOME HONEY!

1
Stand with the feet slightly apart. (The distance between the feet must correspond to that of the pelvis).

2
Bend the knees slightly.

3
Bend the elbows and keep the hands open with the fingers slightly curved like long claws.

The bear has shown me how to keep perfectly still so that I feel part of Nature.

The TRIDENT
Pose

TRISHULA-ASANA

THANKS TO MY LONG NECK OF A GIRAFFE, THIS IS A POSITION THAT I CAN DO PERFECTLY: IT IS CALLED 'TRIDENT', BECAUSE IT MAKES A SHAPE WITH THREE POINTS. IT'S NOT DIFFICULT, DO AS I DO!
STAND UP WITH YOUR LEGS APART AND YOUR KNEES EXTENDED. NOW SLOWLY LEAN FORWARD UNTIL YOUR HEAD IS RESTING ON THE GROUND AND PLACE THE PALMS OF YOUR HANDS BESIDE IT.

1
Stand up and spread your legs.

2
Breathe out and lean forward.

3
Rest the top of the head on the ground and place the palms of the hands beside the head.

The giraffe taught me how to see the world upside-down!

The Gesture of
GREETING

NAMASKARA MUDRA

YOU SEEM VERY AGILE! YOU CAN CERTAINLY IMITATE MY GREETING. SQUAT ON THE GROUND BESIDE ME, BALANCING ON YOUR FEET, WITH THE FEET WIDE APART. BREATHE IN RESTING YOUR ELBOWS ON THE INNER PART OF YOUR KNEES AND BRING YOUR PALMS TOGETHER, SO THAT THEY ARE AT THE LEVEL OF YOUR HEART. BREATHE OUT, EXTEND YOUR ARMS AND LEAN FORWARD, BETWEEN YOUR LEGS. TRY TO REPEAT MY GREETING, FOLLOWING THE RHYTHM OF YOUR BREATHING.

1

Squat on the ground with your legs apart, balance on the soles of your feet.

2

When you breathe in, push your elbows towards the inner part of your knees and bring your hands together in front of your chest.

3

When you breathe out, extend your arms, your body and your head between your legs.

The monkey has taught me how to greet with affection around me: we'll meet again when I wake, friends!

The CANDLE Pose

SARVANGA-ASANA

LIE ON THE GROUND BESIDE ME: I WANT TO SHOW YOU HOW TO TRANSFORM YOURSELF INTO A CANDLE THAT CAN LIGHT THE DARK NIGHTS. STRETCH YOUR NECK, SEPARATING YOUR EARS FROM YOUR SHOULDERS AS FAR AS POSSIBLE. BRING YOUR KNEES UP TO YOUR FOREHEAD AND LIFT YOUR PELVIS, SUPPORTING IT WITH YOUR HANDS. WHEN YOU FEEL STABLE, EXTEND YOUR LEGS, POINTING YOUR FEET TOWARDS THE SKY. CAN YOU FEEL THE STRENGTH FLOWING THROUGH YOUR BODY? IMAGINE THAT IT REACHES YOUR FEET, LIGHTING THEM LIKE THE FLAME OF A CANDLE THAT ILLUMINATES THE DARKNESS.

1
Lie down
and stretch out.

2
Breathe out and give a small
push to lift the pelvis from
the ground. Bring the knees
towards the forehead. Support
the pelvis with the hands.

3
Extend legs and feet towards
the ceiling. The hands will
support the back
and the elbows will be as
close together as possible.

The horse has taught me not to be afraid of the dark, because there will always be a little light inside me.

The PLOUGH
Pose

HALA-ASANA

NOW THAT YOU KNOW THE CANDLE POSE, TRY TO TRANSFORM IT INTO MY FAVORITE POSE. IT IS CALLED 'THE PLOUGH', THE TOOL THAT FARMERS USE TO PREPARE AND TURN THE SOIL BEFORE THEY PLANT NEW SEEDS. IT ISN'T DIFFICULT. STARTING FROM THE CANDLE POSE, DROP YOUR FEET BEYOND YOUR HEAD, UNTIL THEY TOUCH THE GROUND. EXTEND YOUR KNEES AND PLACE YOUR ARMS ON THE FLOOR. IF YOU WANT, YOU CAN USE YOUR ARMS TO SUPPORT YOUR BACK.

1
From the candle pose, let the feet drop beyond the head.

2
Touch the floor with the tips of the toes and extend the knees.

3
Stretch the arms along the floor, or rest the back on the hands for support. Take long, slow breaths.

In this position, I saw my good intentions for the coming day.

The FISH Pose

MATSYA-ASANA

THE FISH POSE IS REALLY FUN: DO YOU WANT TO TRY IT WITH ME? FIRST OF ALL, WE LIE ON OUR BACKS, LEGS TOGETHER AND FEET STRETCHING DOWNWARDS. WE BRING OUR HANDS UNDER OUR BUTTOCKS; WE PUSH OUR ELBOWS INTO THE GROUND AND ARCH OUR BACKS, RISING FROM THE FLOOR. WE PUSH OUR HEADS BACKWARDS UNTIL THE TOP IS RESTING ON THE GROUND. WE TAKE DEEP BREATHS, LIKE A LITTLE FISH THAT HAS REACHED THE IMMENSE OCEAN.

1	2	3
Lie on the ground, bring the legs together and stretch the feet downwards.	The palms of the hands touch the ground, under the buttocks. The elbows press on the ground.	Arch the back and raise it, except for the pelvis and the legs. Tip the head back and rest the top on the ground.

The little fish has taught me to open my heart to the most beautiful dreams.

The TWEEZERS Pose

PASCIMOTTANA-ASANA

SIT DOWN NEXT TO ME SO THAT I CAN SHOW YOU A POSITION THAT RELAXES ME AFTER A LONG DAY IN THE JUNGLE. EXTEND YOUR LEGS IN FRONT OF YOU. BREATHE IN DEEPLY AND THEN, HOLDING YOUR BREATH, STRETCH YOUR ARMS TOWARDS THE SKY. NOW LET THE AIR OUT SLOWLY, WHILE YOU LEAN FORWARD TO GRAB YOUR FEET. NOW, STRETCH FORWARD AS FAR AS POSSIBLE AND TRY TO TOUCH YOUR KNEES WITH YOUR FOREHEAD.

1
Sit on the floor with the legs out and the knees extended.

2
Raise the arms above the head, breathing deeply.

3
Breathe out, leaning forward to grab the feet. Bring the forehead as close to the knees as possible.

Like a tiger, with every breath I try to relax more and more. . .

The ARROW Pose

BANA-ASANA

GET INTO THE CROUCHING POSITION, LIKE ME. TAKE CARE THAT YOUR HANDS ARE IN LINE WITH YOUR SHOULDERS AND YOUR KNEES ALIGNED WITH YOUR PELVIS. NOW YOU ARE A PERFECT ZEBRA, ALL YOU NEED ARE SOME STRIPES!

LIFT YOUR RIGHT ARM AND EXTEND IT. LIFT YOUR LEFT LEG AND EXTEND IT. STRETCH THE ARM AND LEG IN THE OPPOSITE DIRECTIONS, KEEPING THEM PARALLEL TO THE GROUND. REPEAT WITH THE LEFT ARM AND RIGHT LEG. THIS POSITION IS CALLED 'ARROW', BUT LOOKING AT YOU, I THINK OF THE HANDS OF A CLOCK. BY THE WAY, IT IS GETTING LATE. . .

1

Get into a crouching position.

2

Lift the right arm and the left leg.
Stretch them out parallel to the ground.
Repeat with the left arm and right leg.

The zebra thinks that my arms are the hands of a clock that is telling us it is time for bed!

The MOUNT MERU
Pose

MERU-ASANA

WHILE YOU ARE ON FOUR LEGS, I CAN SHOW YOU ONE OF MY FAVORITE POSITIONS. IT TAKES ITS NAME FROM A SACRED MOUNTAIN THAT MANY PEOPLE BELIEVE IS THE CENTER OF THE UNIVERSE! DO YOU WANT TO CLIMB TO THE TOP OF THE MOUNTAIN? THERE MUST BE A WONDERFUL VIEW FROM UP THERE! COME WITH ME. PUSH YOUR FEET INTO THE GROUND AND LIFT YOUR KNEES FROM THE FLOOR. PUSH YOUR HEELS DOWN AND YOUR HIPS TOWARDS THE SKY. EXTEND YOUR KNEES AND ELBOWS.

1
Crouch down and push the feet against the ground.

2
Raise the knees from the floor. Extend the knees and the arms, keeping the back as flat as possible.

I feel tired but I am happy to have climbed Mount Meru with my friend the fox.

The THREE-LEGGED DOG
Pose

EKA PADA ADHO MUKHA SVANA-ASANA

IT TAKES A LITTLE TIME TO READ THE INDIAN NAME OF THIS POSE! LET'S TRY AND SAY IT TOGETHER: EKA PADA ADHO MUKHA SVANA-ASANA. NOW, DO IT WITH ME. FROM THE MOUNT MERU POSE, EXTEND THE LEFT LEG, RAISING IT AND DRAWING AN IMAGINARY DIAGONAL LINE FROM THE LEFT FOOT TO THE HANDS. HOLD THE POSITION FOR A FEW BREATHS AND THEN REPEAT ON THE OTHER SIDE.

1

From the Monte Meru pose,
raise the left leg and extend it.

2

Find balance with the leg
raised and extended. Repeat
on the right side of the body.

The dog has taught me
to find my balance
with calm and patience.

The RESTING WARRIOR Pose

VAJRA-ASANA

EVEN THE STRONGEST AND BRAVEST WARRIORS NEED TO REST; I CAN ASSURE YOU. I WILL SHOW YOU WHAT THEY DO. SIT ON YOUR HEELS WITH YOUR BACK STRAIGHT AND YOUR HANDS ON YOUR THIGHS. CLOSE YOUR EYES AND LISTEN TO YOUR CALM BREATHING.

1

Sit on the heels.

2

Straighten the back and rest the hands on the thighs. Count for how many breaths it is possible to remain calm and immobile.

I too, like every great warrior, sometimes have to stop and rest.

The COW
Pose

GOMUKHA-ASANA

EVERYONE THINKS I AM A CALM AND QUITE ANIMAL, AND YOU KNOW WHAT? THEY ARE RIGHT! THERE IS NOTHING FOR IT; I LIKE A MEADOW FULL OF FLOWERS THAT I CAN ENJOY QUIETLY. THANKS TO MY CALM, I CAN TAKE UP A POSE THAT LOOKS COMPLEX, BUT IF YOU FOLLOW MY INSTRUCTIONS, IT WON'T BE DIFFICULT! SIT WITH YOUR LEGS CROSSED ONE OVER THE OTHER AND YOUR FEET UNDER THE OPPOSING BUTTOCK, ON THE SAME LINE. EXTEND YOUR RIGHT ARM TOWARDS THE SKY, BREATHE IN AND FOLD YOUR LEFT ARM BEHIND YOUR BACK. WHILE YOU ARE BREATHING OUT, BEND YOUR RIGHT ELBOW AND CLASP YOUR HANDS TOGETHER. REPEAT ON THE OPPOSITE SIDE, INVERTING THE POSITION OF YOUR LEGS AND ARMS.

1

Sit on the floor. Cross the legs and place each foot under the opposing buttock, on the same line.

2

Extend the right arm upwards. Bend the left arm behind the back and try to clasp the hands together.

3

Repeat the position on the opposite side. Remember to invert the position of your legs and arms.

In this position, I feel calm and relaxed, like the cows when they are grazing in the mountains.

The HALF-MOON
Pose

ARDHA-CHANDRA-ASANA

LOOK OUT OF THE WINDOW: THE MOON LOOKS LIKE A BOW AND IT'S VERY BRIGHT, ISN'T IT? LET'S TRY TO TAKE UP THE SAME POSITION. SIT ON YOUR HEELS, WITH YOUR BACK VERY STRAIGHT. KNEEL UP AND EXTEND YOUR RIGHT LEG. BREATHE IN, RAISING YOUR LEFT ARM, BREATH OUT, LEANING RIGHT AND LETTING YOUR RIGHT HAND SLIDE DOWN YOUR LEG. THE OTHER ARM WILL DRAW A CRESCENT MOON HIGH IN THE SKY. NOW REPEAT THE POSE ON THE OTHER SIDE!

1

Sit on the heels,
then kneel,
breathing in.

2

Breath out, raising
the right leg, while the left
arm is raised to the sky.
The right foot and the left
leg must be in line.

3

Lean to the right, forming
a half-moon with the body.

This pose brings me the quiet and the peace of the night.

The Pose of the
SAGE MATSYENDRA

ARDHA MATSYENDRA-ASANA

COME AND SIT BESIDE ME AND I WILL TELL YOU A BEDTIME STORY. ONCE UPON A TIME THERE WAS A CURIOUS LITTLE FISH, WHO SAW THE GOD SHIVA REVEAL TO HIS BRIDE PARVATI ALL THE SECRETS OF YOGA. WHEN SHIVA NOTICED THE LITTLE FISH, HE TRANSFORMED HIM INTO A MAN. FROM THAT TIME ONWARDS, MATSYENDRA—THAT WAS HIS HUMAN NAME—BECAME A MASTER OF YOGA, ONE WHO TRANSMITTED TO MAN ALL THE SECRETS OF THIS DIVINE PRACTICE. A RATHER COMPLICATED POSE IS DEDICATED TO HIM. LISTEN AND I WILL TEACH IT TO YOU. SIT ON THE GROUND WITH YOUR LEGS EXTENDED BEFORE YOU. BEND YOUR RIGHT LEG AND PLACE YOUR FOOT ON THE GROUND BEYOND YOUR LEFT KNEE. BEND THE LEFT LEG, PLACING THE FOOT NEAR THE RIGHT BUTTOCK. NOW TURN THE BODY TO THE RIGHT. EXTEND THE LEFT ARM, PUSHING AGAINST THE RIGHT KNEE AND PASS THE ARM UNDER THE KNEE. TRY TO GRASP THE RIGHT HAND BY FOLDING THE ARM BEHIND THE BACK. NOW, LET'S REPEAT THE POSE ON THE OTHER SIDE!

1

Sitting on the floor with the legs extended, place the right foot on the ground, beyond the left knee and bend the left leg inwards.

2

Straighten the back and with the left arm touch the outside of the right knee, as the body turns to the right.

3

Look backwards and try to bring the hands together. . . the body should have formed a knot.

By tying my body in a knot, I release all the tensions of the day!

The STAR
Pose

SAVA-ASANA

SOMETIMES EVEN I DON'T WANT TO GO TO SLEEP, YOU KNOW. I DON'T WANT TO SAY GOODNIGHT AND STOP PLAYING, BUT I HAVE AN IDEA: LET'S GO TO SLEEP TOGETHER, REMAINING CLOSE. LIE ON YOUR BACK WITH YOUR LEGS SPREAD AND YOUR ARMS OUT, LIKE A STAR. TURN THE PALMS OF YOUR HANDS UPWARDS AND CLOSE YOUR EYES. RELAX YOUR BODY; LET IT SINK INTO THE GROUND, WHILE YOU TAKE SLOW, DEEP BREATHS.

VISUALIZATION

PUT ME ON YOUR STOMACH AND WATCH YOUR BREATHING. IF YOU REMEMBER HOW TO COUNT BACKWARDS, COUNT FROM 10 TO 1, WITH LONG, DEEP BREATHS WHILE YOUR STOMACH MOVES IN AND OUT. THE RHYTHM OF YOUR BREATHING WILL SEND ME TO SLEEP WITH A SMILE.

1

Lie down with the palms of
the hands upwards.

2

Extend the arms and legs and close
the eyes. Relax completely to become
a little star in the sky.

When my little friend has gone to sleep, I will follow him to the world of dreams and we can go on playing together.

Regarding
THE SEQUENCES . . .

Although the book is destined for very small children, we want parents to understand that the yoga positions have a value and an energetic quality that goes well beyond the playful aspect. For this to happen, however, the sequence must be organized in a very precise manner, where every position has a meaning and the order is not random—it must be respected. We propose the bedtime yoga sequence, which can also be practiced by adults, so that everyone can experience its value by carrying out all the poses, from the first to the last.

1-Mountain, 2-Bear, 3-Trident, 4-Greeting, 5-Candle, 6-Plough, 7-Fish, 8-Tweezers, 9-Arrow, 10-Mount Meru, 11-Three-legged dog, 12-Resting warrior, 13-Cow, 14-Half-moon, 15-Sage Matsyendra, 16-Star

LORENA V. PAJALUNGA

(Swami Pragya Chaksu Saraswati) thirty years ago she received from her master Swami Satyananda of the Bihar School of Munger Yoga in India, the task of teaching yoga to children. She founded the Associazione Italiana Yoga Bambini (AIYB), now a first level university Master at the Faculty of Educational Sciences. She teaches yoga at the workshop GiocaYoga® and at the Chair of Pedagogy of the Body at the Bicocca University in Milan. In recent years, she has written a number of books for White Star Kids, showing enthusiasm and creativity, including for this series "Play Yoga, Have Fun and Grow Healthy and Happy!"

ANNA LÁNG

Anna Láng is a Hungarian graphic designer and illustrator who is currently living and working in Milan. After attending the Hungarian University of Fine Arts in Budapest, she graduated as a graphic designer in 2011. She worked for three years with an advertising agency, at the same time working with the National Theatre of Budapest. In 2013 she won the award of the city of Békéscsaba at the Hungarian Biennale of Graphic Design with her Shakespeare Poster series. At present she is working passionately on illustrations for children's books. In recent years she has brilliantly illustrated a number of titles for White Star Kids, including, for this series, "Play Yoga, Have Fun and Grow Healthy and Happy!"

WHITE STAR KIDS

White Star Kids® is a registered trademark property of White Star s.r.l.

© 2018 White Star s.r.l.
Piazzale Luigi Cadorna, 6 - 20123 Milan, Italy
www.whitestar.it

Translation and Editing: Iceigeo, Milan (Katherine M. Clifton/Elena Rossi)

ISBN 978-88-544-1270-5
1 2 3 4 5 6   22 21 20 19 18

Printed in Italy by Rotolito - Seggiano di Pioltello (MI)